ISBN 978-81-909760-5-3

Wondrous Glories of Vraja

From Sri Bhakti-ratnākara
of Śrīla Narahari Chakravarti Thākura

By
Dr. Sahadeva dasa
B.com., CA., ICWA., PhD
Chartered Accountant

Soul Science University Press
www.vedictexts.com

Readers interested in the subject matter of this book are invited to correspond with the publisher at :
SoulScienceUniversity@gmail.com
+91 98490 95990

First Edition: December 2010

Price Rs.60/-

Soul Science University Press

Published by : **Dr. Sahadeva dasa**
for Soul Science University Press

Website by : **E. Karnika Yashwant** (Ens.org.in)

Printed by : **Rainbow Print Pack**
Hyderabad

To order a copy write to chadra@rgbooks.co.in or buy online: www.rgbooks.co.in

Dedicated to....

His Divine Grace A.C.Bhaktivedanta Swami Prabhupada

"If one takes shelter of Vṛndāvana under Vṛndāvaneśvarī, Śrīmatī Rādhārāṇī, certainly all the problems of his life are solved very easily."

~Srila Prabhupada (Srimad Bhagavatam 4.8.24p)

Preface

There's more to this world than meets the eye. This would certainly be true for a holy place called Mathurā-maṇḍala or Vraja, situated 90 miles east of Indian capital New Delhi. This is the place where Lord Kṛṣṇa appeared 5000 years ago and performed His uncommon pastimes. This place holds special importance to the followers of Vedic religion and millions flock to this region every year.

India's spiritual culture degraded under foreign subjugation and also in post-independence era due to the government's apathy. This neglect was visible in India's temples and holy places. Once vibrant and flourishing, these places became dilapidated and dirty. After India's indepence, the government declared the factories and malls to be India's new temples and synagogues. Western materialism replaced the age old traditional values.

This state of affairs is evident as one lands in this north Indian district. One is greeted by potholed streets, meandering pigs and overflowing drains. But beneath this chaos, under this filthy covering lies the true spiritual form of this transcendental abode. This can be attested by any one who visits this place. There is something here which captures the heart and mind of the visitor and invokes some inexplicable feelings. This explains why it is on international tourism radar even though there is nothing spectacular here, in an external, superficial sense.

Vedic scriptures tell us that true form of such holy places where the Supreme Lord appears can only be seen by self-realized souls. Until we come to that platform, we can take the clue from such great souls. This book is an endeavour in this direction and it presents excerpts of a dialogue which took place 500 years ago between some great devotees namely, Srila Raghava goswami, Srila Srinivas Acharya and Srila Narottama dāsa Ṭhākura. This dialogue appears in the 5th wave of the famous book, Bhakti-ratnākara, authored by Srila Narahari Chakravarti Thakura. This important book is an encyclopedia of vaisnava lore in post-Chaitanya period.

Finally we can say that no other culture or religion can claim a holy land as all-encompassing and intricate as Vraja, the land of Kṛṣṇa. Hundred and fifty years ago, Mathurā's British magistrate-collector, F.S. Growse, a staunch Catholic, noted, "Almost every spot is traditionally connected with some event in the life of Kṛṣṇa or Rādhā." (Mathurā: A District Memoir)

Sahadeva dasa

Dr Sahadeva dasa

1st January 2011
Secunderabad, India

About Sri Bhakti-ratnakar And Its Author

Bhakti-ratnākara means jewel mine or jewel producing ocean of devotion. It was written in the late eighteenth century by Narahari Chakravarti Thakura, who was also known as Ghanashyam Das. He was the son of Vishvanath Chakravarti Thakur's disciple, Jagannath Chakravarti. He was a noted cook at the Govindadeva temple in Vrindavan, where he studied. Narahari gradually became one of the most prolific Gaudiya writers of the period. Bhakti-ratnākara remains his preeminent work, containing fifteen long chapters and 15,019 verses. His other works include Narottam-vilas, a book on life and teachings of Srila Narottama dāsa Ṭhākura.

Historical accounts of Lord Chaitanya and His associates are found in biographical works such as Chaitanya Bhāgavata of Vrindavan Dasa Thakura, Chaitanya Charitamrta of Kṛṣṇa dāsa Kavirāja Goswami and Chaitanya Mangala of Lochana dasa Thakura. But these works do not cover many other important personalities of the era like Lokanātha Goswami, Gopala Bhatta Goswami or Prabodhānanda Sarasvatī. This is where Sri Bhakti-ratnākara steps in. Also the above books definitely do not describe how the flow of pure devotional service as propounded by Sri Rupa was maintained in post-Chaitanya period.

Three stalwart personalities, Srinivas Acharya, Narottama dāsa Ṭhākura and Srila Shyāmananda Paṇḍita appeared on the horizon of Gaudiya Vaisnavism to drive away the darkness that followed the disappearance of Lord Chaitanya and His associates. These great acharyas carried on the legacy of the sankirtan movement and took it to the next level. Bhakti-ratnākara is perhaps the most prominent and widely read work on the lives of these great personalities.

As far as the bona fides of Bhakti-ratnākara are concerned, Srila Bhaktisiddhānta Saraswati Thakur commissioned the Gaudiya Math edition, which means that in general he accepted the book, and he conceded that in terms of topography (in relation to Vrindavan and Navadvipa) and in terms of siddhanta it had much to offer. Moreover, his father and spiritual mentor, Bhaktivinode Thakur, heavily relied on Bhakti-ratnākara in order to restore the important places of Lord Chaitanya's pastimes. Srila Prabhupada, too, quotes Bhakti-ratnākara in dozens of places in his translations and purports.

As far as mainstream academic world is concerned, Bhakti-ratnākara is accepted by the scholars in general also. D.C. Sen recommends this book as the most important history book of the period. B.B. Majumdar, one of this century's foremost authorities on the Gaudiya vaisnavism, concurs:

Narahari Chakravarti was a diligent historian, a fine biographer, an expert in prosody, a painstaking geographer of the areas surrounding Mathurā and Nabadwip....Naṛahari Chakravarti collected the data about the life of Shrinivas Acharya and Narottam Thakur from written records and oral traditions more than a century after the demise of these persons.

Finally we can say that Bhakti-ratnākara is revered as an authorized Vaishnava text describing the lives of the great Vaishnava saints and important holy places.

The present book contains excerpts from the 5th wave of Sri Bhakti-ratnākara, covering verses from no. 40 to 122. We have included the verses in original Bengali script to make the edition more complete and to augment the authenticity of the message.

bhaktiratnākara grantha parama surasa
asvādaha nirantara nā karaha alasa

Bhakti-ratnākara is a storehouse of nectar. Give up lethargy and relish this nectar constantly, twenty-four hours daily.

mahā mahā pāṣaṇḍīre kaila bhakti dāna
e saba prasaṅga āsvādaye bhāgyavāna

The book Bhakti-ratnākara is full of wonderful narrations and it has converted staunch atheists into great devotees. These narrations are relished only by the fortunate souls.

narahari kahe - ei kṛpā kara more
nirantara dubi yena bhaktiratnakare

Narahari begs for mercy to remain forever drowned in the ocean of pure devotion.

~ *The Author of Śrī Bhakti-ratnākara*

Wondrous Glories of Vraja or Mathura-mandala

মথুরা-মণ্ডল এই বিংশতিযোজনে।
ঘুচয়ে পাতক সব যথা তথা স্নানে।।

mathurā-maṇḍala ei viṁśati yojana
ghūcaye pātaka saba yathā tathā snāne

Mathurā-maṇḍala is spread over an area of 20 yojanas (160miles). One who takes his bath anywhere in this area is freed from all his sins.

তথাহি আদিবারাহে—
বিংশতির্যোজনানান্তু মাথুরং মম মণ্ডলম্।
যত্র তত্র নরঃ স্নাতো মুচ্যতে সর্বপাতকৈঃ।।

tathāhi ādi-vārāhe

viṁśatir yojanānāṁ tu māthuraṁ mama maṇḍalam
yatra tatra naraḥ snāto mucyate sarva-pātakaiḥ

In the Ādi-varāha Purāṇa it is said:

My abode, Mathurā-maṇḍala covers an area of 20 yojanas (or 160 miles). A person becomes free from all sins simply by taking a bath anywhere in this area.

যৈছে সূর্যোদয়ে অন্ধকার দূর করে।
যৈছে বজ্রভয়েতে পর্বত কাঁপে ডরে।।
গরুড়ে দেখিয়া যৈছে সর্প পায় ভয়।
যৈছে মেঘঘটা বায়ুস্পর্শে দূর হয়।।
যৈছে তত্ত্বজ্ঞানে দুঃখ না রহে কিঞ্চিৎ।
সিংহে দেখি' যৈছে মৃগ হয়েত কম্পিত।।
তৃণ-পুঞ্জ অগ্নিসংযোগেতে হয় যৈছে।
মথুরা-দর্শনে সর্ব পাপ-ধ্বংস তৈছে।।

yaiche suryodaye andhakāra dūra kare
yaiche bhayete parvata kāṇpe ḍare
garuḍe dekhiyā yaiche sarpa pāya bhaya
yaiche megha ghaṭa vāyu sparṣe dūra haya
yaiche tattva jñāne duḥkha nā rahe kiñcit
siṁhe dekhi' yaiche mṛga hayeta kampita
tṛṇa-puñja agni saṁyogete haya yaiche
mathurā-darṣane sarva pāpa-dhvaṁsa taiche

As darkness is destroyed by the rising of the sun, as mountains tremble in fear of Indra's thunderbolt, as snakes dread the sight of Garuḍa, as clouds are dispersed by high wind, as lamentations and sorrows disappear with the dawn of knowledge, as wild animals are frightened in presence of a lion and as heaps of straw are burned to ashes by fire, similarly all the sinful reactions of a living entity are destroyed by the sight of Mathurā.

তথাহি আদিবারাহে—

সূর্যোদয়ে তমো নশ্যেৎ যথা বজ্রভয়ান্নগাঃ।
তার্ক্ষ্যং দৃষ্টা যথা সর্পা মেঘা বাতহতা ইব।।
তত্ত্বজ্ঞানাদ্‌যথা দুঃখং সিংহং দৃষ্টা যথা মৃগাঃ।
তথা পাপানি নশ্যন্তি মথুরাদর্শনাৎ ক্ষণাৎ।।

tathahi ādi-vārāhe:

sūryodaye tamo naśyeta
yathā vajra-bhayān nagāḥ
tārkṣyat dṛṣṭvā yathā sarpā
meghā vāta-hatā iva

tattva-jñānad yathā duhkhaṁ
siṁhaṁ dṛṣṭvā yathā mṛgāḥ
tathā pāpāni naśyanti
mathurā-darśanāt kṣaṇāt

Ādi-varāha Purāṇa confirms this statement about Mathurā:

As darkness is vanquished by the sun rise, as elephants fear the goad, as snakes are afraid of Garuḍa, as clouds are scattered by the wind, as unhappiness is destroyed by knowledge, and as deer tremble in front of a lion, so are the sinful reactions destroyed by the sight of Mathurā.

অন্যদ্‌যথা পাদ্মে পাতালখণ্ডে হরগৌরী-সংবাদে—
যথা তৃণসমূহন্তু জলয়ন্তি স্ফুলিঙ্গকাঃ।
তথা মহান্তি পাপানি দহতি মথুরাপুরী।।

anyad yathā pādme pātāla khaṇḍe hara-gaurī-saṁvāde

yathā tṛṇa-samūhaṁ tu jalayanti sphuliṅgikāḥ
tathā mahānti pāpāni dahati mathurā-purī

In the Pātāla-khaṇḍa of Padma Purāṇa, in a conversation between Śiva and Pārvati, the same is confirmed:

As sparks set grass on fire, so does Mathurā-purī destroys even the most grievous sins of living beings.

বিংশতিযোজন এই মথুরামণ্ডলে।
পদে পদে অশ্বমেধযজ্ঞ-পুণ্য মিলে।।

viṁśati yojana ei mathurā-maṇḍale
pade pade aśvamedha-yajña-puṇya mile

Each and every step taken within the 20 yajanas of Mathurā gives the same pious result as that of performing an asvamedha fire sacrifice.

তথাহি আদিবারাহে—
বিংশতির্যোজনানান্তু মাথুরং মম মণ্ডলম।
পদে পদেঽশ্বমেধীয়ং পুণ্যং নাত্র বিচারণম্।।

tatha hi ādi-vārāhe

viṁśatir yojanānāṁ tu
māthuraṁ mama maṇḍalam
pade pade 'śvamedhīyaṁ
puṇyaṁ nātra vicāraṇam

Ādi-varāha Purāṇa states:

My abode, the district of Mathurā is 20 yojanas (160 miles) in size. With every step there one attains the piety of performing an aśvamedha fire-sacrifice. Of this there is no doubt.

জ্ঞানে বা অজ্ঞানেতে যে পাপ উপার্জয়।
অন্যত্র কৃত সে পাপ মথুরা নাশয়।।

jñāne vā ajñānete ye pāpa upārjaya
anyatra kṛta se pāpa mathurā nāśaya

Knowingly or unknowingly, at different times and places, we commit sinful activities. Reactions of all these sinful activities are destroyed in Mathurā.

তথাহি আদিবারাহে—
অন্যত্র হি কৃতং পাপং মথুরায়াং বিনশ্যতি।
জ্ঞানতোঽজ্ঞানতো বাপি যৎ পাপং সমুপার্জিতম্।।

tatha hi ādi-vārāhe

anyatra hi kṛtaṁ pāpaṁ
mathurāyāṁ vinaśyati
jñānato 'jñānato 'vāpi
yat pāpaṁ samupārjitam

As stated in Ādi-varāha Purāṇa:

Whatever sinful reactions one may have accrued in the past, knowingly or unknowingly, anywhere in this world, are all destroyed in Mathurā

বহুজন্মার্জিত পাপ মথুরা বিনাশে।
মথুরামহিমা সর্বপুরাণে প্রকাশে।।

bahu-janmārjita pāpa mathurā vināśe
mathurā mahimā sarva-purāṇe prakāśe

Sinful activities, accumulated over many life-times, are destroyed by the power of Mathurā. Glories of this holy place is described in all the purāṇas.

পাদ্মে পাতালখণ্ডে—
বহুজন্মানি পাপানি সঞ্চিতানি নিবর্তন্তে।
মথুরাপ্রভবং পাপং নশ্যতি ক্ষণমাত্রতঃ।।

pādme pātāla-khaṇḍe

bahu-janmāni pāpāni sañcitāni nivartante
mathurā-prabhavam pāpaṁ naśyati kṣaṇa-mātrataḥ

According to Pātāla-khaṇḍa of Padma Purāṇa, accumulated stocks of sinful activities from many, many births are vanquished in a moment by the influence of Mathurā.

মথুরায় কৈলে পাপ মথুরা নাশয়ে।
স্থিতি হৈলে ধর্ম-অর্থ-কাম-মোক্ষ পায়ে।।

mathurāya kaile pāpa mathurā nāśaye
sthiti haile dharma-artha-kāma-mokṣa pāye

Sins committed in Mathurā are destroyed in Mathurā itself. By residing in Mathurā, a person achieves all necessities of human life namely, religiosity, economic development, sense gratification and liberation.

তথাহি বায়ুপুরাণে—
মথুরায়াং কৃতং পাপং মথুরায়াং বিনশ্যতি।
ধর্মার্থ-কাম-মোক্ষাখ্যং স্থিত্বা তত্র লভেন্নরঃ।।

tatha hi vāyu purāṇe -

mathurāyāṁ kṛtaṁ pāpaṁ mathurāyāṁ vinaśyati
dharmārtha-kāma-mokṣākhyaṁ sthitvā tatra labhen-naraḥ

According to the Vāyu Purāṇa: Any sin committed in Mathurā is destroyed in Mathurā itself. By living in Mathurā one can also attain the four material perfections of human life namely, religiosity, economic development, sense gratification and salvation.

অন্যত্র প্রারব্ধ পাপ ভুঞ্জে দশ বর্ষ।
মথুরাতে সে পাপ ভুঞ্জয়ে দিন দশ।।

anyatra prārabdha pāpa bhuñje daśa varṣa
mathurāte se pāpa bhuñjaye dina daśa

Sins for which one has to suffer for 10 years elsewhere, are vanquished within 10 days in Mathurā.

তথাহি পাদ্মে পাতালখণ্ডে—
অন্যত্র দশভির্বর্ষৈঃ প্রারব্ধং ভুজ্যতে তু যৎ।
কিল্বিষং তন্মহাদেবি মাথুরে দশভির্দিনৈঃ।।

tathahi pādme pātāla khaṇḍe

anyatra daśabhir varṣaiḥ
prārabdhaṁ bhujyate tu yat
kilbiṣaṁ tan mahā-devi
māthure daśabhir dinaiḥ

The Pātāla-khaṇḍa of Padma Purāṇa says: O goddess, sins that fester for 10 years in other places are destroyed in Mathurā in 10 days.

সর্বতীর্থ অধিক শ্রীমথুরা নিশ্চয়।
কৃষ্ণপ্রিয় স্থান ঐছে অন্যত্র না হয়।।

sarva tīrtha adhika śrī mathurā niścaya
kṛṣṇa priya sthāna anyatra nā haya

Mathurā is the best of all sacred places. There is no place in three worlds which is as dear to Kṛṣṇa.

তথাহি আদিবারাহে—
ন বিদ্যতে চ পাতালে নান্তরীক্ষে ন মানুষে।
সমন্তু মথুরায়া হি প্রিয়ং মম বসুন্ধরে।। ৬০

tatha hi ādi-vārāhe

na vidyate ca pātāle
nāntarīkṣe na mānuṣe
samaṁ tu mathurāyā hi
priyaṁ mama vasundhare

In the Ādi-varāha Purāṇa it is said:

O goddess Earth, neither in hell, heaven, nor in the world of humans, is there any sacred place equal to Mathurā. This is my dearmost abode.

ভারতবর্ষেতে ফল মিলে বহু দিনে।
সে ফল মিলয়ে এই মথুরা-স্মরণে।।

bhārata varṣete phala mile bahu dine
se phala milaye ei mathurā-smaraṇe

The result obtained by many years of spiritual endeavor in India is obtained simply by remembering Mathurā.

তথাহি স্কান্দে মথুরাখণ্ডে নারদবাক্যম্—
ত্রিংশদ্বর্ষসহস্রাণি ত্রিংশদ্বর্ষ-শতানি চ।
যৎ ফলং ভারতে বর্ষে তৎ ফলং মথুরাং স্মরন্।।

tatha hi skānde mathurā-khaṇḍe nārada vākyam

triṁśad-varṣa-sahasrāṇi
triṁśad-varṣa-śatāni ca
yat phalam bhārate varṣe
tat phalaṁ mathurāṁ smaran

Śrī Nārada says in Mathurā-khaṇḍa of skanda Purāṇa:

The pious result attained by three thousand years or thirty thousand years of endeavor in the holy land of India is attained by simply remembering Mathurā once.

যে না দেখি' মথুরা দেখিতে যেবা চায়।
যথা তথা মৈলে সে মাথুরে জন্ম পায়।।

ye nā dekhi mathurā dekhite yeba cāya

yathā tathā maile se māthure janma pāya

A person who yearns to see Mathurā and he is unable to do so for some reason and dies without fulfilling this desire, he will be born in Mathurā in next life.

তথাহি পাদ্মে পাতালখণ্ডে—
ন দৃষ্টা মথুরা যেন দিদৃক্ষা যস্য জায়তে।
যত্র তত্র মৃতস্যাস্য মাথুরে জন্ম জায়তে।।

tathahi pādme pātāla-khaṇḍe

na dṛṣṭā mathurā yena
didṛkṣā yasya jāyate
yatra tatra mṛtasyāpi
māthure janma jāyate

In Pātāla-khaṇḍa of Padma Purāṇa it is stated:

If someone cherishes the hope of visiting Mathurā but never gets the opportunity to do so and dies with this unfulfilled hope , he will surely attain a birth in Mathurā in next life.

সর্বশ্রেষ্ঠ শ্রীমথুরা বহু তীর্থাশ্রয়।
মথুরাতে তীর্থ যত সংখ্যা নাহি হয়।।

sarva-śreṣṭha śrī mathurā bahu tīrthāśraya
mathurāte tīrtha yata saṅkhyā nāhi haya

Śrī Mathurā is the best of all places in this universe and it is the shelter of countless holy places. No one can count the number of holy places situated within Mathurā.

তথাহি আদিবারাহে—
ষষ্টিকোটিসহস্রাণি ষষ্টিকোটি শতানি চ।

তীর্থসংখ্যা চ বসুধে মথুরায়াং ময়োদিতা।।

tathāhi ādi-vārāhe

ṣaṣṭi-koṭi-sahasrāṇi
ṣaṣṭi-koṭi-śatāni ca
tīrtha-saṅkhyā tu vasudhe
mathurāyāṁ mayoditā

In the Ādi-varāha Purāṇa it is said: O Earth-goddess, I have indicated 60 thousand millions and 60 hundred million sacred places that reside in Mathurā-maṇḍala.

তথাহি স্কান্দে মথুরাখণ্ডে—
রজসাং গণনা ভূমেঃ কালেনাপি ভবেন্নৃপ
মাথুরে যানি তীর্থানি তেষাং সংখ্যা ন বিদ্যতে।।

tathāhi skānde Mathurā-khaṇḍe

rajasāṁ gaṇanā bhūme
kālenāpi bhaven nṛpa
māthure yāni tīrthāni
teṣāṁ saṅkhyā na vidyate

In the Mathurā-khaṇḍa of Skanda Purāṇa it is stated:

O King, in the course of time it may be possible to count the particles of dust on the earth, but it will not be possible to count the number of holy places in Mathurā.

মথুরা নিবাস সর্ব্ব শাস্ত্রে উপদেশে।
সর্ব্বসিদ্ধি হয় এই মথুরা-নিবাসে।।

mathurā nivāsa sarva śāstre upadeśe
sarva-siddhi haya ei mathurā-nivāse

All scriptures instruct us to reside in Mathurā. One attains all perfections in life simply by residing in Mathurā.

কুরু ভো কুরু ভো বাসং মাথুরীয়াং পুরীং প্রতি।
যত্র গোপ্যশ্চ গোবিন্দস্ত্রৈলোক্যস্য প্রকাশকঃ।।

kuru bhoḥ kuru bho vāsaṁ
māthurīyām purīṁ prati
yatra gopyaś ca govindas
trailokyasya prakāśakaḥ

In the Padma Purāṇa, Pātāla-khaṇḍa, it is said:

O friends, do live in Mathurā Purī, do reside in Mathurā Purī ! This is the eternal abode of Govinda, the creator of three worlds, and His beloved cowherd girls.

রে রে সংসারমগ্নাঢ্য শিক্ষামেকান্ততঃ শৃণু।
যদীচ্ছসি সুখং সান্দ্রং বাসং কুরু মধোঃ পুরে।।

re re saṁsāra-magnāḍhya
sikṣām ekāṁ tu me śṛṇu
yadīcchasi sukhaṁ sāndraṁ
vāsaṁ kuru madhoḥ pure

O friends, plunged in this fearful ocean of birth and death, please listen to this one advice: if you desire intense transcendental bliss, then please reside in Mathurā.

যে মথুরা ত্যজি' করে স্পৃহা অন্যত্রেতে।
সে অতি পামর মুগ্ধ প্রভুর মায়াতে।।

ye mathurā tyaji' kare spṛhā anyatrete
se ati pāmara mugdha prabhura māyāte

One who gives up Mathurā and becomes attached to another place, is a most abominable person and certainly deluded by the illusory potency of the Supreme Lord.

তথাহি আদিবারাহে—

মথুরাঞ্চ পরিত্যজ্য যোঽন্যত্র কুরুতে রতিম্।
মূঢ়ো ভ্রমতি সংসারে মোহিতো মম মায়য়া।।

ata evā di-vārāhe

mathurāṁ ca parityajya
yo 'nyatra kurute ratim
mūḍho bhramati saṁsāre
mohito mama māyayā

Another quote from Ādi-varāha Purāṇa says:

One who leaves Mathurā and finds happiness in some other place is a great fool. He is bewildered by My illusory potency and continuously wanders in the cycle of repeated birth and death.

তথাহি স্কান্দে মথুরাখণ্ডে চ—

মথুরামপি সংপ্রাপ্য যোঽন্যত্র কুরুতে স্পৃহাম্।
দুর্ব্বুদ্ধেস্তস্য কিং জ্ঞানমজ্ঞানেন বিমোহিতঃ।।

tathāhi skānde Mathurā-khaṇḍe

mathurāṁ api samprāpya
yo 'nyatra kurute spṛhām
durbuddhes tasya kiṁ jñānam
ajñānena vimohitaḥ

A similar verse is quoted from Skanda Purāṇa:

He who, although having attained Mathurā, desires to go somewhere else, is a crook with a polluted intelligence. What knowledge can he possibly have since he is bewildered by ignorance.

যার কোন গতি নাই সর্ব্ব প্রকারেতে।
মথুরা তাহার গতি—বিদিত শাস্ত্রেতে।।

yāra kona gati nāi sarva prakārete
mathurā tāhāra gati - vidita śastrete

One who is completely forsaken and forlorn in this world, Mathurā is his only shelter. This is emphatically declared in all the scriptures.

তথাহি আদিবারাহে—
মাত্রা পিত্রা পরিত্যক্তা যে ত্যক্তা নিজবন্ধুভিঃ।
যেষাং কাপি গতির্নাস্তি যেষাং মধুপুরী গতি।।

tathāhi ādi-vārāhe

mātrā pitrā parityaktā
ye tyaktā nija-bandhubhiḥ
yeṣāṁ kvāpi gatir nāsti
teṣāṁ madhu-purī gatiḥ

In the Ādi-varāha Purāṇa it is said:

For them who have been abandoned by family, friends and relatives, and who have no other shelter and nowhere to go, Mathurā is their only shelter and refuge.

সারাৎ সারতরং স্থানং গুহ্যানাং গুহ্যমুত্তমম্।
গতিমন্বেষমাণানাং মথুরা পরমা গতিঃ।।

sārāt sārataraṁ sthānaṁ
guhyānāṁ guhyam uttamam
gatim anveṣamānānāṁ
māthure paramā gatiḥ

Mathurā is the ultimate, confidential abode which lies beyond this material world. It contains the essence of all holy places and it is the supreme destination for the transcendentalists who are searching for the Absolute Truth, the goal of life.

মথুরাতে স্বয়ং কৃষ্ণস্থিতি নিরন্তর।
সর্ব্বশ্রেষ্ঠ ক্ষেত্র বিস্তারিত মনোহর।।

mathurāte svayaṁ kṛṣṇa sthiti nirantara
sarva-śreṣṭha kṣetra vistārita manohara

Lord Kṛṣṇa eternally stays in Mathurā in person. It is the best of all holy places in the three worlds and is imbued with great transcendental beauty.

তথাহি আদিবারাহে—
মথুরায়াং পরং ক্ষেত্রং ত্রৈলোক্য ন হি বিদ্যতে।
যস্যাং বসাম্যহং দেবি মথুরায়াস্তু সর্ব্বদা।।

tathāhi ādi-vārāhe

mathurāyāṁ paraṁ kṣetraṁ
trailokye na hi vidyate
yasmād vasāmy ahaṁ devi
mathurāyāṁ tu sarvadā

In the Ādi-varāha Purāṇa it is said:

O goddess, there is no place in the three worlds which can match the super-excellence of Mathurā. Therefore I eternally reside there.

তথাহি শ্রীমদ্ভাগবতে চতুর্থস্কন্ধে—
তত্তাত গচ্ছ ভদ্রং তে যমুনায়াস্তটং শুচি।
পুণ্যং মধুবনং যত্র সান্নিধ্যং নিত্যদা হরেঃ।।

tat tāta gaccha bhadraṁ te
yamunāyās taṭaṁ śuci
puṇyaṁ madhuvanaṁ yatra
sānnidhyaṁ nityadā hareḥ

In the fourth chapter of Srimad Bhagavatam (4/8/42) it is stated:

My dear boy, I therefore wish all good fortune for you. You should go to the bank of the Yamunā, where there is a virtuous forest named Madhuvana, and there be purified. Just by going there, one draws nearer to the Supreme Personality of Godhead, who always lives there.

তথাহি বিষ্ণুপুরাণে—
হত্বা চ লবণং রক্ষো মধুপুত্রং মহাবলম্।
শত্রুঘ্নো মথুরা নাম পুরীং যত্র চকার বৈ।।

tathāhi viṣṇu-purāṇe

hatvā ca lavaṇaṁ rakṣo-
madhu-putraṁ mahā-balam
śatrughno mathurāṁ nāma
purīṁ tatra cakāra vai

Viṣṇu Purāṇa says:

A verse in Viṣṇu Purāṇa says: Śatrughna founded the city of Mathurā after killing the powerful demon Lavaṇa, the son of demon Madhu.

শ্রীকৃষ্ণকৃপাতে মথুরাতে রতি হয়।
পুণ্য-দানতপাদিতে অলভ্য নিশ্চয়।।

śrī kṛṣṇa kṛpāte mathurāte rati haya
puṇya-dāna tapādite alabhya niścaya

Only by the causeless mercy of Kṛṣṇa one can develop the

attraction for His abode Mathurā. This attraction can not be achieved on the strength of pious work, charities or austerities etc.

তথাহি আদিপুরাণে—
ন তৎ পুণ্যৈর্ন তদ্দানৈর্ন তপোর্ভিন তজ্জপৈঃ।
ন লভ্যং বিবিধৈর্যাগৈর্লভ্যতে মদনুগ্রহাৎ।।

ādi-vārāhe

na tat-puṇyair na tad-dānair
na tapobhir na taj-japaiḥ
na labhyaṁ vividhair yajñair
labhyte mad-anugrahāt

A verse in the Ādi Purāṇa says:

Not by pious activities, not by giving charities, not by austere practices, not by chanting vedic mantras and neither by performing fire sacrifices is Mathurā attained. It is attained only by My causeless mercy.

শ্রীবিষ্ণু কৃপয়া নূনং তত্র বাসো ভবিষ্যতি।
বিনা কৃষ্ণপ্রসাদেন ক্ষণমাত্রং ন তিষ্ঠতি।।

śrī-viṣṇu kṛpayā nūnaṁ
tatra vāso bhaviṣyati
vinā kṛṣṇa prasādena
kṣaṇa mātraṁ na tiṣṭhati

By the grace of Śrī Viṣṇu one obtains residence in Mathurā. Without His mercy one cannot stay even for a moment there.

তথাহি পাদ্মে উত্তরখণ্ডে—
হরৌ যেষাং স্থিরা ভক্তির্ভূয়সী যেষু তৎকৃপা।
তেষামেব হি ধন্যানাং মথুরায়াং ভবেদ্রতিঃ।।

tathāhi pādme uttara-khaṇḍe

harau yeṣāṁ sthirā bhaktir
bhūyasī yeṣu tat-kṛpā
teṣām eva hi dhanyānāṁ
mathurāyāṁ bhaved ratiḥ

In the Padma Purāṇa, Uttara-khaṇḍa, it is said:

Fortunate are the souls who are firmly situated in rendering loving service to Kṛṣṇa and who have attained His great mercy. Only such blessed souls are inclined to live in Mathurā.

মথুরা লভ্য ভগবদ্ধ্যানাদিতে হয়।
অন্যথা অপ্রাপ্য মধুপুরী সুনিশ্চয়।।

mathurā labhya bhagavad-dhyānadite haya
anyathā aprāpya madhupurī suniścaya

One whose mind is constantly absorbed in Kṛṣṇa in pure love, only such a person can attain the shelter of madhupurī.

তথাহি পাদ্মে নির্ব্বাণখণ্ডে—
যদা বিশুদ্ধাস্তপ-আদিনা জনাঃ
শুভাশ্রয়া ধ্যানধনা নিরন্তরম্।
তদৈব পশ্যন্তি মমোত্তমাং পুরীং
ন চান্যথা কল্পশতৈর্দ্বিজোত্তম।।

tathāhi pādme nirvāṇa-khaṇḍe

yadā viśuddhās tapa-ādinā janāḥ
śubhāśrayā dhyāna-dhana nirantaram
tadaiva paśyanti mamottamāṁ purīṁ
na cānyathā kalpa-śatair dvijottama

In the Nirvāṇa -khaṇḍa of Padma Purāṇa it is said:

O best of the brāhmaṇas, living entities who are purified by austerity and other spiritual practices, whose hearts are filled with auspicious things and who are fixed in constant meditation on Me, only they are able to see my supreme abode known as Mathurā. Others cannot see it in millions of kalpas. (A kalpa is a day of Brahma, consisting of a thousand cycles of four yugas.)

শ্রীমথুরা মোক্ষপ্রদা সর্ব প্রকারেতে।
পুরাণাদি কহে ব্যক্ত, বিদিত জগতে।।

śrī mathurā mokṣa-pradā sarva prakārete
purāṇādi kahe vyakta, vidita jagate

It is well known and confirmed in the Purāṇas, Mathurā is the bestower of liberation in every respect.

তথাহি আদিবারাহে—
যা গতির্যোগযুক্তস্য ব্রহ্মজ্ঞস্য মনীষিণঃ।
সা গতিস্ত্যজতঃ প্রাণান্ মথুরায়াং নরস্য চ।।

tathāhi ādi-vārāhe

yā gatir yoga-yuktasya
brahmajñasya manīṣinaḥ
sā gatis tyajataḥ prāṇān
mathurāyāṁ narasya ca

In the Ādi-varāha Purāṇa it is said:

What the yogis strive for with various asṭānga yoga practices, what the jñānis are trying to achieve by realizing brahman, what the thoughtful philosophers acquire after years of contemplation, all that perfection is easily achieved by a person who leaves his body in Mathurā.

তীর্থে চৈব গৃহে বাপি চত্বরে পথি চৈব হি।
যত্র তত্র মৃতা দেবি মুক্তিং যান্তি ন চান্যথা।।

tīrthe caiva gṛhe vāpi
catvare pathi caiva hi
yatra tatra mṛtā devi
muktiṁ yānti na cānyathā

O goddess, Mathurā is absolute, one may die anywhere within its boundary, either in one's home or at a holy place or in a courtyard or even on a street, he will attain liberation without any doubt.

কাশ্যাদিপুর্য্যো যা হি সন্তি লোকে
তাসান্তু মধ্যে মথুরৈব ধন্যা
আজন্মমৌঞ্জীকৃতমৃত্যুদাহৈ-
র্নৃণাং চতুর্দ্ধা বিদধাতি মোক্ষম্।।

kāśy-ādi-puryo yā hi santi loke
tāsāṁ tu madhye Mathurāiva dhanyā
ā janma-mauñjī-kṛta-mṛtyu-dāhair
nṛṇāṁ caturdhā vidadhāti mokṣam

Among the various holy cities like Kāśī, Mathurā is most auspicious because she bestows liberation upon human beings in four ways: in Mathurā they may attain liberation by birth, by vows of initiation, by death, or by cremation.

কৃমিকীটপতঙ্গাদ্যা মথুরায়াং মৃতা হি যে।
কূলাৎ পতন্তি যে বৃক্ষাস্তেঽপি যান্তি পরাং গতিম্।।

kṛmi-kīṭa-pataṅgādya
mathurāyāṁ mṛta hi ye
kūlāt patanti ye vṛkṣās
te 'pi yānti parāṁ gatim

All living entities who die here in Mathurā district, including insects, worms and moths and even trees which fall with their roots torn up, they all attain the supreme destination.

চাণ্ডালপুক্কসস্ত্রীণাং জীবহিংসারতস্য চ
মথুরাপিণ্ডদানেন পুনর্জন্ম ন বিদ্যতে।।

pādme pātāla-khaṇḍe

cāṇḍāla-pukkasa-strīṇām
jīva-hiṁsā-ratasya ca
mathurā-piṇḍa-dānena
punar janma na vidyate

In the Padma Purāṇa, Pātāla-khaṇḍa, it is said:

If the ceremony of piṇḍa-dāna (offering homage to dead souls) is performed for some one in Mathurā, even though he or she may be an outcaste, an aborigine, a lady or even a sinful murderer, such a person attains freedom from cycle of birth and death.

প্রণাল্যামিষ্টকে চাপি শ্মশানে ব্যোম্নি মঞ্চকে।
অট্টালে বা মৃতা দেবি মাথুরে মুক্তিমাপ্নুয়ুঃ।।

praṇālyām iṣṭake cāpi
śmaśāne vyomni mañcake
aṭṭāle vā mṛto devi
māthure muktim āpnuyuḥ

O goddess, dying anywhere in Mathurā district, whether in a ditch, in a house, at a crematorium, in the sky, on a throne, or in a tower, a living entity attains liberation.

অস্তীহ মথুরা নাম ত্রিষু লোকেষু বিশ্রুতা।
কৃষ্ণপাদরজোমিশ্রবালুকাপূতবীথিকা।।

স্পর্শেন রজসস্তস্যা মুচ্যতে জন্মবন্ধনাৎ।।

astīha mathurā nāma
trīṣu lokeṣu viśrutā
kṛṣṇa-pāda-rajo-miśra-
bālukāpūta-vīthikā
sparśanena naras tasya
mucyate sarva-bandhanāt

Here is glorious Mathurā, famed in three worlds. Its pathways are purified by the dust of Kṛṣṇa's lotus feet. Merely by its touch, people can attain salvation from miseries and bondage of the material world.

তথাহি মথুরাখণ্ডে—
মথুরায়াং বসিষ্যামি যাস্যামি মথুরামহম্।
ইতি যস্য ভবেদ্বুদ্ধি সোঽপি বন্ধাৎ প্রমুচ্যতে।।

tathāhi mathurā-khaṇḍe

mathurāyāṁ vasiṣyāmi
yasyāmi mathurāmhaṁ
iti yasya bhaved buddhiḥ
so 'pi bandhāt pramucyate

In the Mathurā-khaṇḍa it is said:

What to speak of going to Mathurā, even mere desire or thought of going to Mathurā or living in Mathurā is sufficient to guarantee liberation from material world.

বিষ্ণুলোকপ্রদ এই মথুরা-মণ্ডল।
সর্বমতে নাশয়ে জীবের অমঙ্গল।।

Viṣṇuloka-prada ei mathurā-maṇḍala
sarva-mate nāśaye jīvera amaṅgala

Mathurā is a bestower of eternal residence in Viṣṇuloka, the spiritual world. It destroys all the inauspiciousness and miseries in lives of those who seek its shelter.

যে পশ্যন্ত্যচ্যুতং দেবং মাথুরে দেবকীসুতম্।
তে বিষ্ণুলোকমাসাদ্য ক্ষরন্তে ন কদাচন।। ১

ye paśyanty acyutaṁ devaṁ
māthure devakī-sutam
te viṣṇu-lokam āsādya
kṣarante na kadācana

Those who get to see the Deity of Kṛṣṇa, the son of mother Devaki in Mathurā, attain the spiritual world and never return to this material world.

যাত্রাং করোতি কৃষ্ণস্য শ্রদ্ধয়া যঃ সমাহিতঃ।
সর্বপাপবিনির্মুক্তো বিষ্ণুলোকং স গচ্ছতি।।

yātrāṁ karoti kṛṣṇasya
śraddhayā yaḥ samāhitaḥ
sarva-pāpair vinirmukto
viṣṇulokaṁ sa gacchati

A person who celebrates the festivals of Lord Kṛṣṇa in Mathurā with full faith and attention, becomes free from all sinful reactions and goes back home, back to Godhead.

তথাহি পাদ্মে পাতালখণ্ডে—
স্ত্রিয়ো ম্লেচ্ছাশ্চ শূদ্রাশ্চ পশবঃ পক্ষিণো মৃগাঃ।
মথুরায়াং মৃতা যে চ তে যান্তি পরমাং গতিম্।।

tathāhi pādme pātāla khaṇḍe

striyo mlecchās ca śūdras ca paśavaḥ pakṣiṇo mṛgāḥ
mthurāyām mṛtā ye ca te yānti paramāṁ gatiṁ

Padma Purāṇa, Pātāla-khaṇḍa states:

Mathurā awards salvation to all those who leave their bodies within its precincts whether they be women, outcastes, laborers or even birds and beasts.

সর্পদষ্টাঃ পশুহতাঃ পাবকাম্বুবিনাশিতাঃ।
লব্ধাপমৃত্যবো যে চ মাথুরে হরিলোকগাঃ।।

sarpa-daṣṭāḥ paśu-hatāḥ
pāvakāmbu-vināśitāḥ
labdhāpa-mṛtyavo ye ca
māthure hari-loka-gāḥ

Death in Mathurā may be caused by a snake bite, an attack of wild animals, by fire or drowning in water or any other sort of unnatural reasons, but all such living entities dying thus are transferred to Vaikuṇṭhaloka, the abode of Hari.

সর্বাভীষ্টপ্রদ শ্রীমথুরা—শাস্ত্রে কয়।
যার যে কামনা তারে তাহাই মিলয়।।

sarvābhīṣṭa-prada śrī mathurā - śastre kaya
yāra ye kāmanā tāre tāhāī milaya

Scriptures confirm that Mathurā fulfills all the aspirations of a living being, whether material or spiritual. Whatever one desires there, he receives it accordingly without fail.

তথাহি ব্রহ্মাণ্ডপুরাণে—
সত্যং সত্যং মুনিশ্রেষ্ঠ ব্রুবে শপথপূর্ব্বকম্।
সর্বাভীষ্টপ্রদং নান্যন্মথুরায়াঃ সমং ক্বচিৎ।।

tathāhi brahmāṇḍa-purāṇe

satyaṁ satyaṁ muni-śreṣṭha
brūve śapatha-pūrvakam
sarvābhiṣṭa-pradaṁ nānyan
mathurāyāḥ samaṁ kvacit

A verse in the Brahmanda Purāṇa says:

It is true, absolutely true! O great sage, I vow that it can not be otherwise. I assure you that there is no other place in this world quite like Mathurā. It can fulfil all desires of all living beings.

তথাহি স্কান্দে মথুরাখণ্ডে—
ক্ষেত্রপালো মহাদেবো বর্ত্ততে যত্র সর্ব্বদা।
যত্র বিশ্রান্তিতীর্থঞ্চ তত্র কিং দুর্লভং ফলম্।।

tathāhi skānde mathurā-khaṇḍe

kṣetra-pālo mahā-devo
vartate yatra sarvadā
yatra viśrānti-tīrthaṁ ca
tatra kiṁ durlabhaṁ phalam

In the Skanda Purāṇa, Mathurā-khaṇḍa, it is said:

What remains difficult to be obtained in a place like Mathurā which is protected by Lord Śivā himself and where there are holy places like Viśrāma-ghāṭa?

ত্রিবর্গদা কামিনাং চ মুমুক্ষুণাঞ্চ মোক্ষদা।
ভক্তীচ্ছোর্ভক্তিদা সা বৈ মথুরামাশ্রয়েদ্বুধঃ।।

tri-varga-dā kāminām yā
mumukṣūṇāṁ ca mokṣadā
bhaktīcchor bhaktidā sā vai
mathurāṁ āśrayed budhaḥ

What wise man would not seek shelter of Mathurā, which awards the three goals of life (religiosity, wealth and earthly pleaures) to materialists and which grants liberation to they who hanker after liberation, and which bestows devotional service to those who desire devotional service?

শ্রীমথুরামণ্ডল প্রপঞ্চাতীত হন।
কে বর্ণিতে পারে মথুরার গুণগণ।।

śrī mathurā-maṇḍala prapañcātīta hana
ke varṇite pāre mathurāra guṇa-gaṇa

The district of Mathurā is situated beyond this material world of five elements though it appears to be part of it. Who can describe its host of virtues?

তথাহি আদিবারাহে—
অন্যৈব কাচিৎ সা সৃষ্টির্বিধাতুর্ব্যতিরেকিণী।
ন যৎক্ষেত্রগুণান্ বক্তুমীশ্বরোঽপীশ্বরো যতঃ।।

tathāhi ādi-vārāhe

anyaiva kācit sā sṛṣṭir
vidhātur vyatirekiṇī
na yat kṣetra-guṇān vaktum
īśvaro 'pīśvaro yataḥ

The Ādi-varāha Purāṇa states:

As even the Lord Himself cannot describe all the super-excellent qualities of Mathurā, this place must be a special creation of Providence.

তন্মণ্ডলং মাথুরং হি বিষ্ণুচক্রোপরিস্থিতম্।
পদ্মাকারং সদা তত্র বর্ত্ততে শাশ্বতং নৃপ।।

tan-maṇḍalaṁ māthuraṁ hi
viṣṇu-cakropari sthitam
padmākāraṁ sadā tatra
vartate śāśvataṁ nṛpa

In the Skanda Purāṇa, Mathurā-khaṇḍa, it is said:

O King, this transcendental abode of Mathurā is shaped like a lotus and it is situated on the chakra of Viṣṇu and it shall never perish.

দেবত্রয়রূপ শ্রীমথুরা মনোহিত।
মাথুরশব্দের অর্থ পুরাণে বিদিত।।

devatraya-rūpa śrī mathurā manohita
māthura-śabdera artha purāṇe vidita

Mathurā is the form of the Trinity - Brahmā, Viṣṇu and Śiva. The Purānās describe the meaning of word Mathurā.

তথাহি পাদ্মে পাতালখণ্ডে—
মকারে চ থুকারে চ রকারে চান্তসংস্থিতে।
নিষ্পন্নো মথুরা শব্দ ওঁকারস্য ততঃ সমঃ।।

tathāhi pādme pātāla-khaṇḍe

ma-kāre ca thu-kāre ca
ra-kāre cānta-saṁsthite
niṣpanna māthuraḥ śabda
oṁ-kārasya tataḥ samaḥ

The Padma Purāṇa, Pātāla-khaṇḍa, again states:

The name Mathurā is equal to the sound of aum (oṁkāra). As Mathurā contains the letters Ma, u, and a, so does the word aum. These three syllables make up the name of Mathurā.

মহারুদ্রো মকারঃ স্যাৎ থুকারো বিষ্ণুসংজ্ঞকঃ।
রকারোঽন্তস্থো ব্রহ্মা স্যাৎ ত্রিশব্দং মাথুরং ভবেৎ।।

mahā-rūdro ma-kāraḥ syād
thu-kāro viṣṇu-saṁjñakaḥ
ra-kāro 'ntastho brahmā syāt
tri-śabdaṁ māthuraṁ bhavet

The word Ma represents Mahārudra Śiva; thu represents Viṣṇu; and ra represents Brahmā. In this way the word Mathurā represents the three deities, Brahmā, Viṣṇu, and Śiva.

অতঃ শ্রেষ্ঠতমং ক্ষেত্রং সত্যমেব ভবত্যুত।
সা ত্রিদেবময়ী মূর্ত্তির্মথুরা তিষ্ঠতে সদা।।

ataḥ śreṣṭha-tamam kṣetram
Satyameva bhavaty uta
sā tri-devamayī mūrtir
māthurī tiṣṭhate sadā

This is absolutely true and there is not the least exaggeration in the statement that Brahmā, Viṣṇu, and Śiva always reside in Mathurā in the form of deities.

শ্রীমদ্বিষ্ণুভক্তি মথুরাতে লভ্য হয়।
বিবিধ প্রকারে নানা পুরাণেতে কয়।।

śrīmadviṣṇu-bhakti mathurāte labhya haya
vividha prakāre nana purāṇete kaya

All auspicious devotional service unto the Lord can easily be obtained in Mathurā. This fact is explained in different ways in different Purāṇas.

অন্যেষু পুণ্যক্ষেত্রেষু মুক্তিরেব মহাফলম্।
মুক্তৈঃ প্রার্থ্যা হরেভক্তির্মথুরায়াস্তু লভ্যতে।।

pādme uttara-khaṇḍe

anyeṣu puṇya-kṣetreṣu
muktir eva mahā-phalam
muktaiḥ prārthya harer bhaktir
mathurāyāṁ tu labhyate

In the Padma Purāṇa, Uttara-khaṇḍa it is said:

In other holy places, liberation is the greatest reward one can achieve. But in Mathurā one can gain what is prayed for by the liberated—devotional service to Lord Hari.

ত্রিরাত্রমপি যে তত্র বসন্তি মনুজা মুনে।
হরির্দদ্যাৎ সুখং তেষাং মুক্তানামপি দুর্লভম্।।

tri-rātram api ye tatra
vasanti manujā mune
harir dadyāt sukhaṁ teṣāṁ
muktānām api durlabham

O great sage, to they who spend even three nights in Mathurā, Lord Hari bestows on them that which even the liberated souls cannot attain. (ie.,precious divine love)

ত্রৈলোক্যবর্ত্তিতীর্থানাং সেবনাদ্দুর্লভা হি যা।
পরানন্দময়ী সিদ্ধির্মথুরাস্পর্শমাত্রতঃ।।

brahmāṇḍa-purāṇe

trailokya-varti-tīrthānāṁ
sevanād durlabhā hi yā
parānandamayī siddhir
mathurā-sparśa-mātrataḥ

In the Brahmāṇḍa Purāṇa it is said:

The precious attainment of ecstatic love, which is rarely obtained by serving all the holy places in the three worlds, can easily be attained simply by touching the dust of Mathurā.

স্মরন্তি মথুরাং যে চ মথুরেশং বিশাম্পতে।
সর্ব্বতীর্থফলং তেষাং স্যাচ্চ ভক্তিহরৌ পরে।।

smaranti mathurāṁ ye cā
māthureśaṁ viśāmpate
sarva-tīrtha-phalaṁ teṣāṁ
syāc ca bhaktir harau parā

The Skanda Purāṇa, Mathurā-khaṇḍa, states: O King, those who constantly remember Mathurā and the King of Mathurā [Kṛṣṇa], attain devotional service unto the lotus feet of Lord Hari which is the end result of all pilgrimages to all holy places.

স্বতো মথুরা পরমফল বিতরয়।
হেন মথুরায় কেবা না করে আশ্রয়?

svato mathurā parama-phala vitaraya
hena mathurāya kebā nā kare āśraya?

This merciful abode bestows the highest benediction on the living entities. What person in this world would not not seek its shetler?

তথাহি পাদ্মে পাতালখণ্ডে—
অহো মধুপুরী ধন্যা বৈকুণ্ঠাচ্চ গরিয়সী।
দিনমেকং নিবাসেন হরৌ ভক্তিঃ প্রজায়তে।।

tathāhi pādme pātāla-khaṇḍe

aho madhu-purī dhanyā
vaikuṇṭhāc ca garīyasī
dinam ekaṁ nivāsena
harau bhaktiḥ prajāyate

In the Padma Purāṇa, Pātāla-khaṇḍa, it is said:

Oh what a glorious place is Mathurā! It is better than Vaikuṇṭhā in every respect. Anyone who spends even a day in Mathurā will attain devotion to the lotus feet of Śrī Hari.

আদিবারাহে—
যদীচ্ছেৎ পরমাং সিদ্ধিং সংসারস্য চ মোক্ষণম্।
মথুরা গীয়তাং নিত্যং কর্মণা মনসাপি চ।।

yadīcchet paramāṁ siddhiṁ
saṁsārasya ca mokṣaṇam
mathurām gīyatām nityam
karmaṇa manasāpi ca

If one yearns for the supreme perfection and release from the cycle of birth and death, he should constantly glorify Mathurā with his body, mind, and words.

THE AUTHOR

Dr. Sahadeva dasa (Sanjay Shah), is a monk in vaisnava tradition. Coming from a prominent family of Rajasthan, India, he graduated in commerce from St.Xaviers College, Kolkata and then went on to complete his CA (Chartered Accountancy) and ICWA (Cost and works Accountancy) with national ranks. Later he received his doctorate.

For close to last two decades, he is leading a monk's life and he has made serving God and humanity as his life's mission. His areas of work include research in Vedic and contemporary thought, Corporate and educational training, social work and counselling, travelling in India and aborad, writing books and of course, practicing spiritual life and spreading awareness about the same. He is also the President of ISKCON Secunderabad since almost twenty years.

He is also an accomplished musician, composer, singer, instruments player and sound engineer. He has more than a dozen albums to his credit so far. (SoulMelodies.com) His varied interests include alternative holistic living, Vedic studies, social criticism, environment, linguistics, history, art & crafts, nature studies, web technologies etc.

His earlier books, Oil - A Global Crisis and Its Solutions (oilCrisisSolutions.com), End of Modern Civilization and Alternative future (WorldCrisisSolutions.com) have been acclaimed internationally.

OTHER BOOKS BY THE AUTHOR

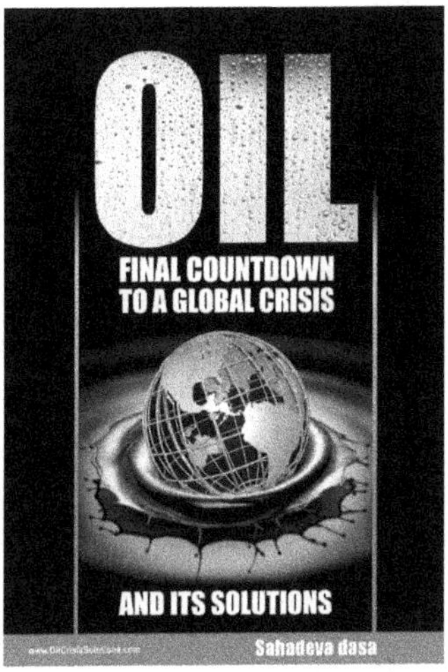

This unique book by the author examines the lifeline of modern living - petroleum. In our veins today, what flows is petroleum. Every aspect of our life, from food to transport to housing, its all petroleum based. Either its petroleum or its nothing. Our existence is draped in layers of petroleum. This book is a bible on the subject and covers every conceivable aspect of it, from its strategic importance to future prospects. Then the book goes on to delineate important strategic solutions to an unprecedented crisis thats coming our way.

Pages-330, www.OilCrisisSolutions.com
For a copy, write to: soulscienceuniversity@gmail.com

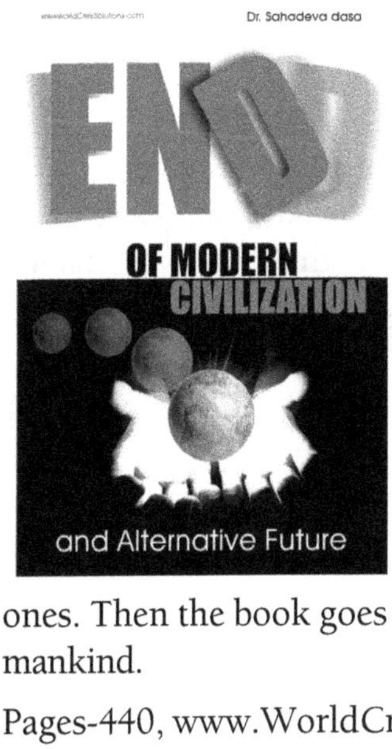

This book by Dr Sahadeva dasa is an authoritative work in civilizational studies as it relates to our future. Dr. dasa studied human civilizations of last 5000 years and the reasons these civilizations went into oblivion. Each of these civilizations collapsed due to presence of one or two factors like neglect of soil, moral degradation, leadership crisis etc. But in our present civilization, all the factors that brought down all the these civilizations are operational with many more additional ones. Then the book goes on to chalk out the alternative future for mankind.

Pages-440, www.WorldCrisisSolutions.com
For a copy, write to: soulscienceuniversity@gmail.com

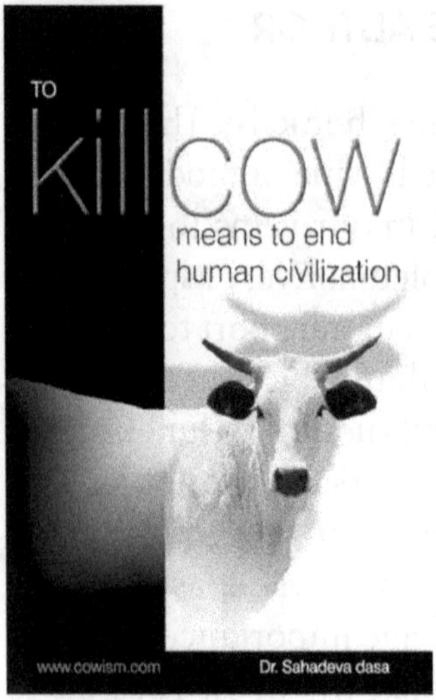

This landmark book on cow protection delineates various aspects of cow sciences as presented by the timeless voice of an old civilization, Vedas. This book goes on to prove that the cow will be the making or breaking point for humanity, however strange it may sound. Science of cow protection needs to be researched further and more attention needs to be given to this area. Most of the challenges staring in the face of mankind can be traced to our neglect in this area.

Pages-136, www.cowism.com

For a copy, write to: soulscienceuniversity@gmail.com

This book discusses the vital role of cows in peace and progress of human society. Among other things, it also addresses the modern ecological concerns. It emphasizes the point that 'eCOWlogy' is the original God made ecology. For all the challenges facing mankind today, mother cow stands out as the single answer.

Living with cow is living on nature's income instead of squandering her capital. In the universal scheme of creation, fate of humans has been attached to that cows, to an absolute and overwhelming degree.

Pages-144, www.cowism.com

For a copy, write to: soulscienceuniversity@gmail.com

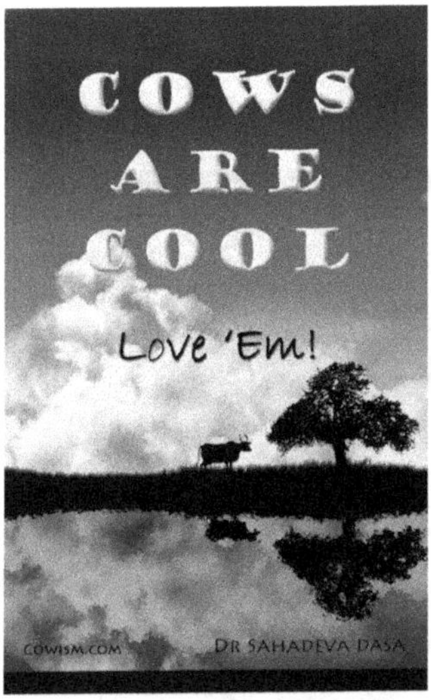

This book deals with the internal lives of the cows and contains true stories from around the world. Cow is a very sober animal and does not wag its tail as often as a dog. This does not mean dog is good and cow is food. All animals including the dog should be shown love and care. But cow especially has a serious significance for human existence in this world. Talk about cows' feelings is often brushed off as fluffy and sentimental but this book proves it otherwise.

Pages 136, www.cowism.com
For a copy, write to: soulscienceuniversity@gmail.com

Music Albums: Free Downloads From
Soul Melodies.com

Music Albums: Free Downloads From Soul Melodies.com

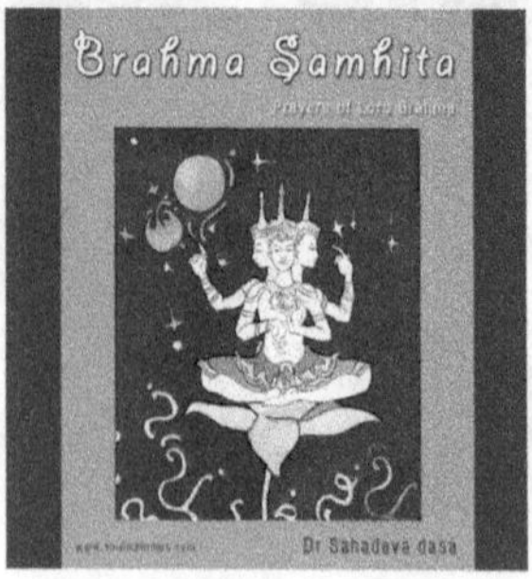

www.ingramcontent.com/pod-product-compliance
Lightning Source LLC
Chambersburg PA
CBHW060544030426
42337CB00021B/4421